P9-DJA-423

"**Is there anyone among us** who has not, at one time or another, felt the pain and frustration for not being appreciated for who they really are? *A Peacock in the Land of Penguins*, a powerful message, simply told, speaks to the spirit in each of us that yearns to fly high and free."

— LAURIE BETH JONES
author of *Jesus, CEO* and *The Path*

"**Every sworn and nonsworn member** of the Los Angeles Police Department who participates in our Department's day-long Cultural Diversity Training program leaves with a personal copy of *A Peacock in the Land of Penguins*. This lighthearted little book reinforces the spirit of understanding and appreciation that we are trying to encourage in the LAPD."

— WILLIE L. WILLIAMS
Chief of Police, Los Angeles Police Department

"**Back in those early days at NBC,** when the ratings weren't too stellar, and I would often feel the icy stare of general managers at Affiliate meetings — I thought of *myself* as the Peacock in the Land of Penguins!"

— BRANDON TARTIKOFF
"Media Mogul and Living Legend," formerly with
NBC, Paramount, and New World Entertainment

"**Your new book is charming,** pertinent and should be a big hit — I hope it is. Congratulations!"

— CONNIE KOENENN
Staff Writer, *Los Angeles Times*

"**What a wonderful book!** It offers a cautionary tale for managers and executives everywhere about the meaning and importance of diversity for successful businesses today. It should be required reading!"

— BOB NELSON
author of *1001 Ways to Reward Employees*
and *Managing for Dummies*

"**I have been part of 'penguin' organizations** and watched disasters result from lack of management diversity. They would have saved tens of millions by paying attention to this simple little book."

— JAMES B. SHAFFER
President and CEO, Guy Gannett Communications,
a diversified media holding company, Portland, Maine

"**This is certainly an insightful book,** which looks into some of the corporations I have been a part of, as well as others with which I am not familiar. It is 'right on' and tells us a lot about ourselves — things we sometimes don't want to know."

— LARRY STRUTTON
Publisher, *Rocky Mountain News,* Denver, Colorado

"***A Peacock in the Land of Penguins* made me laugh and cry.** I laughed as you so simply revealed the 'bottom line' about my experience at my previous company. I cried for all the valuable years I lost trying to become a penguin."

— LINDA SINILA
California mortgage broker

"A little book full of big ideas, that went a long way in helping us change the conversation around teamwork at EDC. We have used it at all levels, and truly talk about the Land of Opportunity! Merci BJ et Warren!"

— MARIE-LYNE LEMAIRE
Manager, Training and Development,
Export Development Corporation, Ottawa, Ontario, Canada

"I very much enjoyed your book, *A Peacock in the Land of Penguins,* and have made copies available to our senior management team. I highly recommend all corporate executives take fifteen minutes of their time to read your book."

— MIKE LAMOTHE
Executive Director, Human Resources,
Merck Frosst Canada, Quebec

"Congratulations on giving us a new motto: "E Pluribus Maximus!" (Greatness from Many!) This is a commandment for today's organizations."

— BARRY Z. POSNER
coauthor of *The Leadership Challenge* and *Credibility*

"Introducing diversity issues through personalized 'bird' characters is a wonderful gift. It makes the core concepts and feelings easily accessible without creating resistance — the first critical step in the process of learning to relate effectively across individual and group differences to create personal, interpersonal, and organizational synergy."

— LEWIS GRIGGS
coauthor of the book *Valuing Diversity;* Executive Producer of three video series "Valuing Diversity," "Valuing Relationship," and "Human Energy at Work," as well as the CD-ROM series "No Potential Lost"

"**This book offers great insights** into what's necessary to effectively value and manage differences in the workplace. It helps people understand the dynamics of diversity and challenges us to embrace the opportunities that diversity brings us."

— HAROLD W. BURLINGAME
Executive Vice President, AT&T

"**Management books abound.** They describe corporate cultures and assess workforce diversity. Few, however, have the impact of this fable about the rich results that can be obtained when a diverse workforce is freed from conformist pressures, and valued for the unique contributions of its members."

— JANE PISANO
Dean, School of Public Administration,
and Vice President, External Relations,
University of Southern California

"*A Peacock in the Land of Penguins* **is a wonderful fable** for individuals and organizations striving to flourish in a diverse world. While it may ruffle some feathers, a valuable message is delivered with wit and humor."

— PHYLLIS PFEIFFER
Publisher, *Marin Independent Journal*,
Gannett Newspapers

"**Insightful and witty** . . . Hateley and Schmidt have captured an essential truth about navigating the stormy sea of the contemporary workplace — from the strength of differences we can truly make a difference."

— JIM KOUZES
coauthor of *The Leadership Challenge* and *Credibility*,
and President of the Tom Peters Group

"A Peacock in the Land of Penguins is a poignant, creative tale
of real life in a world full of differences that's dominated by a
majority striving for sameness — a brilliant, delightful fable
that captures the essence of diversity in organizations."

— DAVID W. JAMIESON, Ph.D.
coauthor of *Managing Workforce 2000:
Gaining the Diversity Advantage*

"A light-hearted treatment of a difficult problem, this story
reminds us of what we are really after in our diversity efforts."

— ANN M. MORRISON
author of *Breaking the Glass Ceiling* and
*The New Leaders: Guidelines on Leadership
Diversity in America*

"A Peacock in the Land of Penguins is an effective tool** in
teaching students diversity. By communicating in metaphors,
it puts the topic of tolerance in simple terms, which are not
restricted to specific racial biases. I've personally used the
book in a variety of settings, including university classrooms,
as well as corporate seminars."

— RICHARD G. WONG
Manager, Training and Development,
Orange County Transportation Authority

"It's a clear, straightforward explanation of what Diversity is
all about, presented in cheerful terms. It's nicely done!"

— DR. FRANCINE RILEY
Executive Director, Workforce Diversity, GTE

"*A Peacock in the Land of Penguins* is a beautiful metaphor that goes to the heart of diversity issues and concerns. The added quiz, checklists, how-to's, practical tips and suggestions in the revised edition are important aids to anyone interested in working with and understanding diversity from a fresh perspective. It's a must-read!"

— PHILLIP R. WALKER, Ph.D.
Walker International, Inc., Workforce Diversity Consultant
to NASA Lewis Research Center

"I loved it! This is an engaging tale of the challenges and dilemmas faced by those who are "different" as they struggle for success and fulfillment — as well as the challenges and dilemmas of those who are members of the power elite in today's organizations. Truly a fable for our times!"

— DR. JUDY B. ROSENER
author of *America's Competitive Secret: Utilizing Women as a Management Strategy,* and coauthor of *Workforce America! Managing Employee Diversity as a Vital Resource*

A peacock IN THE LAND OF **PENGUINS**

A Tale of Diversity and Discovery

Barbara "BJ" Hateley
and Warren H. Schmidt

Illustrations by Sam Weiss
Foreword by Ken Blanchard

Berrett-Koehler Publishers
San Francisco

Copyright © 1995, 1997 by Barbara "BJ" Hateley

All rights reserved. No part of this publication may be reproduced, distributed, or transmitted in any form or by any means, including photocopying, recording, or other electronic or mechanical methods, without the prior written permission of the publisher, except in the case of brief quotations embodied in critical reviews and certain other noncommercial uses permitted by copyright law. For permission requests, write to the publisher, addressed "Attention: Permissions Coordinator," at the address below.

Berrett-Koehler Publishers, Inc.
450 Sansome Street, Suite 1200
San Francisco, CA 94111-3320
Tel: (415) 288-0260   Fax: (415) 362-2512

ORDERING INFORMATION

Individual sales. Berrett-Koehler publications are available through most bookstores. They can also be ordered direct from Berrett-Koehler at the address above.

Quantity sales. Special discounts are available on quantity purchases by corporations, associations, and others. For details, contact the "Special Sales Department" at the Berrett-Koehler address above.

Orders for college textbook/course adoption use. Please contact Berrett-Koehler Publishers at the address above.

Orders by U.S. trade bookstores and wholesalers. Please contact Publishers Group West, 4065 Hollis Street, Box 8843, Emeryville, CA 94662. Tel: (510) 658-3453; 1-800-788-3125. Fax: (510) 658-1834.

Printed in the United States of America

 Printed on acid-free and recycled paper that is composed of 85% recovered fiber, including 15% post-consumer waste.

Library of Congress Cataloging-in-Publication Data

Hateley, B. J. (Barbara J.)
    A Peacock in the Land of Penguins; A Tale of Diversity and Discovery / Barbara "BJ" Hateley and Warren H. Schmidt; illustrations by Sam Weiss; foreword by Ken Blanchard. — 2nd ed. p. cm.
    ISBN 1-57675-010-8 (alk. paper)
    1. Pluralism (Social sciences) — Fiction. I. Schmidt, Warren H.
    II. Title.
    PS3358.A7378P43 1997
    813'.54–dc21   97-11540
                                                          CIP

Second Edition
05 04 03 02 01 00   12 11 10 9 8 7

Cover and book design: Vinje Design, Inc., San Francisco, CA

A Note from the Authors
about this Expanded Edition

When we first began writing this parable about a peacock in the Land of Penguins several years ago, little did we know where the book would ultimately take us! We knew we had an important message about individuality and conformity in the context of today's organizations — and we wanted to express it in a way that would entertain as well as enlighten. We wanted to write a story that would speak to both the hearts and minds of people.

However, we had no idea how popular the book would become, and that it would evolve into a veritable cottage industry — with translations into many languages worldwide, a bestselling video that would be used in conferences and seminars, assessment instruments for consultants and trainers, and a whole world of merchandising — a game, T-shirts, coffee mugs, penguin pens, etc!

Since its first publication in January 1995, many of our readers have let us know that they were hungry for more information — ideas and suggestions about what to DO with the insights from our book. "How can I deal with my own situation?" they would ask us.

This expanded version is our answer to their questions. In addition to the original parable, we have added "Tips and Tools for Feathered Friends" — as a resource for both individuals and organizations. We hope you will find it helpful!

Barbara "BJ" Hateley
Warren H. Schmidt
Los Angeles, California
January, 1997

Foreword

Every once in a while a small book comes along that deals with a profound subject in a very simple, elegant way. *A Peacock in the Land of Penguins* is such a book. It brings new insight into the much-discussed issue of diversity in the workplace – and it does so in a most engaging manner. Through the medium of a fable, this book helps us to see what can happen when we try to express ourselves fully and courageously in an environment created by executives and managers who view the world very differently.

This is the story of Perry the Peacock – a bright, talented, colorful bird – who comes to live in the Land of Penguins. He soon runs into problems because the penguins have established a chilly organizational climate that is formal, bureaucratic, and governed by a vast array of written and un-written rules. Although his talent is recognized, his different and unusual style makes the penguins feel uneasy. His experience reflects that of "birds of a different feather" in many of today's organiza-tions. While the gospel of "valuing diversity" is preached in seminars and meeting rooms through-out American business, government, education, and religious institutions, the rhetoric does not always match the reality.

Being "different" is much more than a matter of race and gender. Diversity in its fullest sense involves a broad range of human uniqueness – personality, work style, perception and attitudes, values and lifestyle, work ethic, world view, communication style, and much more. Valuing diversity means appreciating and encouraging people to be who they really are, helping them to develop their full potential, and utilizing their special talents, skills, ideas, and creativity.

This delightful corporate fable, based on the experiences of real people, follows the adventures of Perry the Peacock and other exotic birds as they try to make their way in the Land of Penguins. Their story is both entertaining and enlightening. This is a tale of the perils and possibilities of being "different" in a world that values comfort, safety, and the predictability of conformity.

Anyone involved in an organization – executives, human resource people, managers and supervisors, and employees – should read this little book. There are important insights for all of us!

Ken Blanchard

Acknowledgments

This book reflects the creative thoughts of many minds and the encouragement of many hearts. This page mentions only a few of those to whom we owe so much . . .

First and foremost, we wish to thank Margret McBride, without whose early and continued support, encouragement, and editorial suggestions this book would not have been completed. We are deeply grateful for her guidance throughout every step of the creative process.

Steven Piersanti, our publisher, is very much a kindred spirit and a joy to work with. It has indeed been a creative partnership, and his thoughtful suggestions helped us to refine and polish our work. Steve and his team at Berrett-Koehler have invested much time and energy in helping us get our story into final format. We look forward to continued collaboration and a fruitful future.

And Sam Weiss, who turned out to be much more than an illustrator, helped bring our characters to life. In the process, he enriched our project with his thoughtful insights, questions, and comments. We appreciate the way his own "peacock" nature shines through his drawings!

We also wish to thank the real-life "exotic birds," as well as the "penguins," whose experiences inspired our corporate fable. They will undoubtedly recognize themselves and the roles they played in the Land of Penguins. Extra thank-you's go to Phyllis Pfeiffer, Jim Shaffer, Larry Strutton, and Jeff Hall, whose inspiration, critiques, and feed-back were especially helpful.

And finally, a very special thanks to our families, especially Reggie Schmidt, Michael Hateley and Gloria Gallagher, who provided continuous support, encouragement, and helpful critiques as our fable took shape. Their love and attention nurtures our creative spirits.

BJH & WHS

There once was a time,
in the not so distant past,
when penguins ruled many lands
in the Sea of Organizations.

These penguins were not always wise,
they were not always popular,
but they were always in charge.

Most organizations looked the same:

Top executives
and managers
wore their distinctive penguin suits,
while worker birds
of many kinds
wore colors and outfits
that reflected their work
and their lifestyles.

Birds who aspired to move up
in their organizations
were encouraged to become
as penguin-like as possible —
to shorten their steps
and learn the penguin stride,
to wear penguin suits,
and follow
the example of their leaders.

Employee Development Departments
offered
extensive training programs
on
appropriate penguin-like behavior.

The rules
and norms
were clear
from Day One.

Penguins advised in subtle
(and not so subtle) ways:

"This is the way we do things here."

"If you want to be successful,
be like us."

Some of the birds
who wanted to move up
in the pecking order
became very good
at taking on the penguin look
and penguin behaviors.

But even *they*
found that
they never quite
made it
into key positions.

It was assumed by all
that penguins
were natural leaders —
orderly, loyal, and good team players.

Penguins could be trusted
to put
the organization's interests
ahead
of personal and family concerns.

Other birds
were thought to be
more flighty
and less dependable.

Of course,
this was never stated
out loud
or in writing.

Because,
like every organization,
penguins wanted to be seen
as fair-minded and
ready to promote
on the basis of
talent,
hard work,
and contribution.

But everyone really knew —

The penguins
had always been in charge,
and
the penguins
would *always be in charge.*

The elder penguins
would take
younger penguins
under their wings
and coach them
on
how to be successful.

They would invite them
to play golf
and go jogging.

They would sit together
in the executive dining room
and talk about sports.

*It was clear to everyone
who the important penguins were.*

*It was also clear
that the penguins
felt most comfortable
around each other.*

Life was harmonious
in the Land of Penguins,
as long as everyone played
by the penguins' rules.

The other birds
in the organization
knew how to act
to make the penguins
feel comfortable
and secure.

But there came a time
when things began to change
in the Land of Penguins . . .

Senior penguins
would visit
other lands,
where they encountered
interesting birds
who impressed them
with their
management talent,
experience,
and accomplishments.

"These birds are not penguins,"
the elders thought,
"but perhaps
they could become penguins
if we brought them to our land
and trained them
in our penguin ways."

"Surely
these impressive and unusual birds
could adapt to life
in the Land of Penguins,
and the talent
they bring
would make us
even more successful."

"Our climate is different —
chilly and cold.
And our terrain is unique —
icy and barren.

"But we have thrived there
and so perhaps
will these new birds.

"If they are as smart
as we think they are,
they can adjust
to our weather and our ways."

And this was how
Perry the Peacock
came to live
in the Land of Penguins . . .

.

N_{ow}
Perry was clearly
not a penguin.

In fact,
he was the antithesis of penguinity —

Perry was a peacock —
a bright, colorful, and noisy bird.

Perry was a very talented peacock,
who had accomplished
some very impressive things
in his own land.

He could write well
and was excellent
at managing his budgets.
He was creative and imaginative,
and at the same time,
practical and sensible.

He had many friends and admirers
in his own land,
and was very popular and well-liked.

Senior managers
in the Land of Penguins
were intrigued
when they met Perry the Peacock.

They knew that he was different —
but they were impressed
with what he had achieved in his career,
and they were fascinated
with the possibilities
that he represented.

They felt that Perry
had real Penguin Potential.

Perry, in turn,
was attracted to the penguins
because of the great things
he had heard and read
about their land —
the promise of status,
and wealth,
and a sense of belonging
to a great and powerful enterprise.

It was a rich land —
and all the birds
were paid extremely well.

"My future will be brighter,"
he thought,
"in this new land."

And so the penguins
and the peacock
agreed.

He would join them,
and together
they would achieve
great things.

At first
everyone was delighted.

The penguins were pleased
and impressed
with their new recruit.

He stood out
from the crowd
in the way he sparkled
and displayed flashes of color
every now and then.

And Perry was pleased, too,
with the novelty
and the newness.

He was impressed
by the penguins —
they looked so important
in their black and white suits,
especially
when they gathered together
for meetings
and company events.

Their formality and manners
were so different
from anything
he had ever seen
or experienced
before.

Now the peacock
was careful
in the beginning
not to display
too much of his colorful nature.

You see, some friends
in his own land
had warned Perry about penguins —

They had cautioned him
about the rules
and the style
with which the penguins
governed their land.

So he kept his feathers
folded up
much of the time,
and would only occasionally
flash them open
to dazzle the penguins
with the full range of his talent and color.

He wanted
to be taken seriously
and he wanted
to be successful.

So he subdued
his own peacock nature
for a while,
until he could be sure
that the penguins had accepted him
completely.

He was confident
that when he produced
good results for them,
they would embrace him fully —
in all his peacock glory —
and he could relax
and just be himself.

You see,
   things were very different
   in the land where he had grown up —
   in the Land of Learning.

   In the Land of Learning
   there were LOTS of different kinds of birds.

   There were wise birds (owls),
   and powerful birds (eagles),
   and hunting birds (hawks),
   improbable birds (ostriches),
   elegant birds (swans),
   and awkward birds (gooney birds).

It was crowded and noisy,
with a buzz of activity
and the rough and tumble
of competition.

Birds had to work hard,
learn fast,
and live by their wits
and creativity
in order to be successful.

It was an exhilarating
but tough
environment!

The motto in the Land of Learning was:

All the birds
worked hard
to prove their talent
and earn their place
in the sun.

In the Land of Learning
the birds didn't always
get along peaceably.

Sometimes there were
conflicts and differences,
struggles and irritations.

But conflicts and differences
were valued
because the birds believed
that that's how new ideas get tested.

Discussion,
debate,
and argument —
that's the way
change was introduced
and progress was made.

Nobody cared
if you were a penguin or a peacock,
a dove or a bluejay.

Being smart
and talented
and productive
was all that mattered.

Initiative,
creativity,
and results
were most highly prized.

It was what was inside you
and what you contributed
that counted —
not the kind or color
of feathers you wore.

But Perry the Peacock
was in for
some very different challenges
when he left
the Land of Learning
and went to work
in the Land of Penguins.

He was used to hard work
and fighting for his ideas
and competing with
many different kinds of birds.
But nothing in his background
had prepared him for
the unique ways
and special customs
of the Land of Penguins.

He wanted to do well
and be successful.

He was flattered
that these powerful and prestigious penguins
had recruited him
into their ranks,
and he wanted to please them.

He studied the penguins' walk,
their talk,
and their style.

"How strange,"
he thought to himself,
"they all look alike.
They're like clones of each other."

He was intrigued
and puzzled
at the same time.

And as time went on, his troubles began . . .

Some of the penguins
began to grumble
that his distinctive peacock voice
was too loud.

You see,
penguins speak
in very subdued,
modulated
tones,
and the peacock's laughter
and excited exclamations
startled their time-honored
sense of propriety.

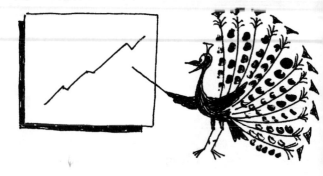

His feathers began to show
more and more all the time,
as he worked hard
and accomplished
many great things.

Everyone agreed
that he was quite talented
and productive,
and they liked the impressive results
of his work.

But his flashy, colorful style
made some
of the senior penguins
uneasy.

Many of the other penguins
in the land
were delighted
with this new and unusual bird
in their midst.

They called him
"a breath of fresh air"
and welcomed his exuberance.

Some of the junior penguins
privately speculated
about how long he would last
in the Land of Penguins.
They saw
how un-penguinlike he was,
and wondered how long
this would be tolerated by the
elders.

A couple of the senior penguins
  tried to take him
  under their wings and coach him.

"Look," they said,
"we like your work,
  but some of the elders
  are uncomfortable with your style."

"You need to change to be accepted here."

"Why don't you put on a penguin suit,
  so you look more like us?"

"It doesn't fit,"
responded Perry the Peacock.

"It's too tight and constraining.
My tail feathers will get crushed
and my wings can't move well."

"I can't work if I'm not comfortable."

The elders said,
"Well then,
maybe you could paint your feathers
black and white,
like ours."

"Then at least
you wouldn't look
quite so different."

"What's wrong with the way I am?"
Perry asked.

He was hurt and confused.

"I work hard,
I produce great results —
everyone says so."

"Why can't you look at my work
rather than my feathers?"

"Aren't my accomplishments
more important
than my style?"

"It's such a small thing,"
the penguins responded.

"You are smart and talented.
You could have a bright future here.
You just need to act
more like us
and then
the elders will be more comfortable."

"You need to wear a penguin suit,
and soften your voice,
and shorten your steps."

"Just watch all the other penguins —
see how they act?"

"Try to be like the rest of us."

Perry believed
that their intentions were good,
but their words wounded him nonetheless.

"Why can't I just be who I am?
Why do I have to change
to be accepted by you?"
he asked.

"That's just the way things are here,"
the penguins shrugged.

"It's the same everywhere
in the Sea of Organizations."

He suspected they might be right,
but his heart didn't want to accept it.

He thanked them
for their words of advice
and their concern for him,
and he went back to his nest
to think things over.

As the months rolled by,
he discussed his dilemma
with some of the other birds he trusted.

Several of them
were also new birds
who had been recruited
around the same time as
Perry's arrival
in the Land of Penguins.

Many of them
were experiencing
similar kinds
of problems . . .

Edward the Eagle
complained that he, too,
was getting pressure
to change.

He was smart and powerful
and very skilled at his work,
and he even wore the requisite penguin suit.

But Edward didn't talk
or act like a penguin,
and this bothered the elders.

They were embarrassed
by his accent,
and sent him to
a prestigious,
tradition-steeped
Eastern Business School
for special executive penguin training.

But it didn't work —
he was still an eagle in penguin's clothing.

He couldn't change who he was.

And Helen the Hawk
had similar problems.

She was beautiful and powerful —
smart, sharp, and aggressive.
She was a skilled hunter,
with fierce competitive instincts.

She wore her penguin suit,
occasionally more colorful
than the male penguins,
but still acceptable.

Helen tried to adapt
to the style of the penguins,
but her hawk-like nature
would always reveal itself.

Her talons were sharp,
her eyes piercing,
her manner intense,
her hunter's instincts
ever alert.

And her aggressive style
made the elders very uncomfortable.

It was the same story
with Mike the Mockingbird.

He was an especially brilliant bird —
creative,
imaginative,
and impulsive.
He was attracted by sparkling ideas.

He flew fast,
worked hard,
and jumped around
making good things happen
all over the Land of Penguins.

But Mike soon discovered that
penguins are territorial birds,
who build their empires,
establish their pecking order,
and fiercely resent anyone
who comes into their turf
without being properly invited.

Since Mike was not a penguin,
he was not sensitive
to the politics
and the turf issues
of the senior penguins.

With his penchant for creativity
and imagining possibilities
outside the ordinary,
he sometimes offended
some of the elders
by flying into their territories.

They were threatened and annoyed
at his intrusions.

Like Edward the Eagle
and Helen the Hawk,
Mike wore his penguin suit
and tried his best
to learn the ways of the penguins
so he would be accepted by them.

But ultimately,
he could not change who he really was.

The story was similar
with Sara the Swan.

She was an optimistic dreamer,
with unusual visions
for the future
of the Land of Penguins.

She had interesting ideas,
unique ideas,
good ideas —

but her ideas
often were not heard
because she expressed them
in such a gentle way.

Her style was graceful,
her manner gracious,
but the penguins
had doubts about
her toughness
and her strength.

VISION

There were others as well . . .

The thing they all had in common
was that none of them
had grown up
in the Land of Penguins.

They had been
recruited and hired
from other places.

The penguin elders
had enticed these outsiders
with promises of success:

"We want your fresh thinking
and new ideas.
We admire your track record
and want you to do
great things for us."

But
as soon as the new birds
were inside the organization,
the elders issued them
penguin suits
and began pressuring them
to talk,
act,
and think
more like penguins.

The penguins said,
"We value diversity."

But their actions said otherwise.

As the exotic new birds
discussed
their mutual frustrations
among themselves,
they tried
to figure out
what to do.

Several of them
decided to try
to change the culture
rather than
let the culture change them.

"We'll work on our bosses,
and other key penguins,"
they vowed,
"without
being too obvious,
of course."

They each
developed strategies
for becoming
Agents of Change
within the Land of Penguins.

Edward the Eagle
adopted a **"Strategy of Support."**

> *"Catch your boss*
> *doing something right . . .*
> *(or approximately right!)"*

Whenever his boss
accepted
any new idea,
Edward would reinforce him
by saying,
"I appreciate
your willingness
to try
something different.
Your support
makes my job
interesting
and rewarding."

Helen the Hawk
had her own ideas
about how to bring about change.
She used a **"Strategy of Hopeful Thinking."**

> *"Act on the basis*
> *of assumptions*
> *you'd **like** to be true . . .*
> *(with caution, of course!)"*

Helen would regularly send
her boss
newspaper clippings
and magazine articles
with a personal note
which read:

"Because
of your continuing interest
in learning new ways
to handle our marketing,
I thought
you'd like to see
the attached article
about
Prosperous Enterprise, Inc.
in the recent issue of
the 'Journal of Successful Organizations.'"

Mike the Mockingbird
decided he would try
an extremely bold strategy —
a **"Strategy of Calculated Ignorance."**

*"Violate
penguin policy —
and if caught —
use the Puzzled Prodigal Response."*

Whenever Mike was questioned
about making a particular decision,
he would assume
an expression of puzzlement
as he described
how a shortcut
would achieve something
that everyone
had agreed
was important.

Sara the Swan,
being much gentler
in her approach,
tried a *"Strategy of Safe Learning."*

"Expose
the Senior Penguins
to new ideas
in settings
where
they won't be embarrassed
by having to respond."

Sara would casually mention
her ideas and suggestions
in quiet conversations
and informal settings.

She "planted ideas,"
nurtured them slowly,
and watched for progress.

Some of the other birds —
who were determined
to transform themselves —
tried very hard
to become penguins.

They walked the penguin walk;
they talked the penguin talk.

They preened
and practiced
to produce the desired result.

But ultimately they failed,
because
they couldn't change
who they really were.

And a few birds,
like Perry,
didn't even try
to become penguins.

Perry just knew
in his heart
that there must be
at least *one* land in
the vast Sea of Organizations
where
he could be a peacock
and be valued
for his uniqueness.

He resisted
the penguins' advice and pressure,
firm in his conviction
that he should be valued
for his results.

Over time,
things got worse
for Perry
and the other exotic birds
in the Land of Penguins . . .

Their strategies
to change
the penguin way of doing things
met with
resistance and red tape.

Their ideas and efforts
were discounted
and dismissed.

Their questions of "Why?"
were answered with:
"This is the way
we've *always* done things here."

The exotic birds learned
through painful experience
that the culture
of the land
was deeply entrenched.

The structures and systems
were rigid and unbending.
Policies and procedures
ensured the continuity
of the penguin practices.

It eventually became clear
that individual efforts
at persuasion and influence
were foolish and futile
in the face of such
longstanding tradition
and structure.

The exotic birds realized
that the penguin ways
had developed
over many years
and would not change
easily or soon.

Their strategies
to change themselves
also fell short,
because
deep down inside
they just weren't penguins.

They couldn't change
who they really were.

Their hearts were filled
with frustration,
disappointment,
and sadness.

They had come
to the Land of Penguins
with such high hopes
and great expectations.

They had wanted to contribute
and be successful.

But what they got instead
was quiet criticism,
stifling conformity,
and subtle rejection.

And so,
one by one,
Perry and the other new birds
each began to realize
the same thing —

*They could not be themselves
in the Land of Penguins.*

They had to move on.

They knew their futures
lay somewhere else
in the vast Sea of Organizations.

Some of the new birds
left the Land of Penguins
on their own.

Others
were pushed out
by the senior penguins,
who said,
"You make us too uncomfortable.
You don't fit here.
You must leave."

Whether they left on their own
or were forced out by the elders,
all the departing birds
shared one thing in common —
the pain and confusion
of being different,
and the sadness
and disappointment
of not being accepted for who they were.

These birds of a different feather
had all struggled
with the same dilemma:

*How much
could they
or would they
change to "fit in"
and be accepted
in the Land of Penguins,
and how much
could they be themselves?*

What price would they pay to be successful?

And the penguins had their own dilemma:

How much diversity
could they tolerate in their land
and still maintain
their own comfort level?

Wouldn't
all these differences
endanger
their harmonious corporate culture?

The penguins,
after all,
had enjoyed
many years of profitable success
by following
historic penguin traditions
and ways of doing business.

They were reluctant
to change the style
that had made them great.

And they were disappointed
that so many
of their new recruits
did not work out.

Perry the Peacock
was the first to leave.

He had many friends
from other lands,
and they told him
of a new and wondrous place
they had visited in their travels.

They described it as
"the Land of Opportunity."

There,
they told him,
his work
and his contributions
would be valued —
and his uniqueness
would be applauded,
not criticized.

He could be
colorful,
flamboyant,
and enthusiastic,
and others would appreciate him
for his distinctive style.

Dare he hope
that these reports were true?

Was this the place
he had longed for?

He had to go
and see for himself.

When Perry arrived in
the Land of Opportunity
he found that it
was totally different
from the Land of Penguins . . .

Here,
workers and bosses
didn't waste
time and energy
pretending to be
something different
from what they were.

They knew
that they needed
many different kinds of birds
in order to thrive
in the turbulent and competitive
Sea of Organizations.

And they knew that
the most important requirement
for organizational success
is acceptance and trust.

It is acceptance and trust
that make it possible
for each bird
to sing its own song —
confident that it will be heard —
even by those
who sing with a different voice.

All the birds
expressed themselves freely,
and their lively exchanges
of differing views
ensured
that their work
and their ways
were constantly improving.

Best of all,
they had confidence
in their leaders,
birds of many kinds
who had risen to
their positions
through talent,
skill,
and ability.

The motto here was:

E PLURIBUS MAXIMUS
(Greatness from Many)

Some birds swam,
many flew,
and some kept their feet
planted firmly on the ground.

This gave them
many different perspectives
on the world —
which they shared
easily and openly
with one another.

Their shared knowledge made them wise.
And their wisdom made them successful.

Perry knew
he had found his new home.

As the months and years
rolled by,
one by one,
Edward the Eagle,
Helen the Hawk,
Mike the Mockingbird,
and Sara the Swan
also made their way
to the Land of Opportunity.

They had heard from Perry
about the freedom
and openness
that existed there.

In this land,
Edward could fly free and high,
soaring as fast
as his wings could carry him.

Others admired
his grace and power —
and commented
on what an inspiration he was
to younger birds
who came from humble beginnings
but had ambitious dreams
of flying high someday themselves.

Nobody even noticed
the way he spoke,
with his unique accent.

Helen,
who had rattled the penguins
with her intensity
and her keen competitive instincts,
found a place
where she was welcome
in the Land of Opportunity.

Her colleagues
valued her hunting skills
and her ability to spot
changing trends
and possibilities
for new ventures.

They commented frequently
on her elegant beauty
and distinctive style.

She was perfectly suited
for her new position
in the Land of Opportunity.

Mike
at long last
experienced the creative joy
of jumping from project to project,
working hard and fast,
and stirring up new ideas
wherever he went.

No longer fettered
by a rigid pecking order
and boundaries
dictated by penguins,
his productivity skyrocketed —
and others marveled
at his amazing skills.

Sara, too,
found the Land of Opportunity
to be a hospitable place
for her dreamy,
reflective,
imaginative
style of working.

She started writing
and pursuing ideas
in ways
she once thought
would never be possible
in a place of work.

Other birds flocked to her,
wanting to work with her
and share
in the realization
of her dreams.

She was appreciated
for the freedom
she allowed others,
and
for her gentle style.

These diverse birds
all prospered and grew
as never before.

They felt affirmed
and appreciated
by the other birds
in the land.

They experienced a new freedom,
allowing them to fly,
each with their own unique style.

They worked hard —
and enjoyed
the fruits of their labors.

Above all else,
they knew the joy of just being themselves.

Perry the Peacock flashed his colorful feathers;

Edward the Eagle soared with power and grace;

Helen the Hawk skillfully kept watch and hunted;

Mike the Mockingbird followed his creative instincts and innovative ideas; and

Sara the Swan drifted and floated with the currents.

Perry and his friends
found that
life was good and
their future was bright
in the Land of Opportunity.

There
they could all succeed —
each with a different style —
and make contributions
that would be welcomed and appreciated
by their colleagues
and coworkers.

*They came to realize
that the Land of Opportunity
is more than a place . . .*

It is a state of mind.

The Land of Opportunity is an attitude.

It is
an openness to new ideas,
a willingness to listen,
an eagerness to learn,
a desire to grow,
and the flexibility to change.

The Land of Opportunity
is a new way of dealing with one another.

It becomes a reality
when we stop judging each other
by superficial criteria
and begin to see
and appreciate
everyone
as uniquely
talented,
capable,
and valuable.

The Land of Opportunity
is where we live and work
when we choose
to see with new eyes,
live from our hearts,
and allow ourselves
and others
to be what we truly are . . .

Ourselves.

The End

Afterword

. . . and what of the Land of Penguins?

Their story continues to unfold every day
in corporations and organizations
across the country . . .

Tips and Tools
for
Feathered Friends

For those who are trying to find the way to their own Land of Opportunity...

Read on and enjoy: **Page**

Are You a Peacock
(or other type of exotic bird)?

YES NO

☐ ☐ 1. Do you frequently feel like you don't "fit in" —
         that you are "different" in some fundamental way?

☐ ☐ 2. Do you get criticized for not being a "team
         player"? ("Team player" being a euphemism for
         conforming to group norms.)

☐ ☐ 3. Do you feel pressured by your boss or others to
         change in some significant way to fit in?

☐ ☐ 4. Do you feel ostracized, lonely, "left out of the loop"
         of information and decision making?

☐ ☐ 5. Are you unable to identify with anyone as a role
         model at the top of your organization?

☐ ☐ 6. Are your ideas and suggestions routinely rejected as
         "not the way we do things here"?

☐ ☐ 7. Do you often feel under- or un-appreciated for your
         talent and skill, while others who are less talented get
         promoted and rewarded?

☐ ☐ 8. Do you often try to figure out "what's wrong with me"?

☐ ☐ 9. Do you feel stifled, stuck, frustrated by some unseen
         "system"?

☐ ☐ 10. Are you frequently ignored, interrupted, or discounted
         when you make comments or suggestions at meetings?

___ ___ **TOTALS**

If you answered "yes" to six or more of these questions, you are
definitely a Peacock or some other type of "exotic bird" in your
organization!

If you answered "yes" to four or five of these questions, you are
probably somewhat ambivalent about where you are working.
In some ways you "fit," and in other ways you struggle.

If you answered "yes" to three or fewer questions, you might be an
exotic bird in the Land of Opportunity, or you might be a
penguin in the Land of Penguins. The point is, you are probably
a pretty good "fit" in your organization.

Survival Tips for Peacocks
(and other exotic birds)
Who Stay Put in the Land of Penguins

1. Don't let your work suffer because you're discouraged about being different. Strive for excellence in all you do. Your professional track record is your most important asset, both inside the Land of Penguins and outside.

2. Seek out other exotic birds (both inside and outside your organization) for friendship, networking, and moral support.

3. Make conscious and careful choices about how much you can and will adapt or change to be successful in the penguins' eyes. What price are you willing to pay? (See "Strategies for Birds of a Different Feather.")

4. Be prepared and flexible enough to put on a penguin suit occasionally when it's necessary and/or important. Think of it as "penguin camouflage."

5. Know that you are not defective — there is nothing wrong with you. Your talent, skill, and ideas are valuable, even if the penguins don't recognize or reward you.

Survival Tips for Peacocks Who Are on the Move, in Search of the Land of Opportunity

1. Be realistic about the world of work. You're going to find some penguins in most organizations, especially the large ones.

2. Try to stay out of organizations that are heavily dominated by penguins. If you're still working in one, keep your eyes open for more diversity-friendly places to work (especially small, entrepreneurial organizations).

3. Consider self-employment as an option. It's not for everyone, but many exotic birds are living happier lives by opting out of mainstream organizations.

4. Take comfort in the fact that you are not alone. There are many, many peacocks and exotic birds who feel the same way you do. Seek them out; ask their advice; take heart in their successes.

5. Be a good example to other exotic birds. Be supportive, help other birds, encourage those who are different to find their way to happiness and success.

Strategies for
"Birds of a Different Feather"

If you are a Peacock or some other exotic bird in your organization, you have options and choices about whether you should stay in your organization or "fly the coop" to another job in another organization, or to self-employment.

If you stay, then you have many choices about how best to survive (maybe even thrive!) in a less than perfect work environment. Each of the strategies described here has its pros and cons. A few of these strategies will seem realistic and "do-able" in your situation. Some may seem inauthentic or distasteful to you. Others may appeal to you, but you're not sure you can carry it off. Still others may be politically dangerous in your organization, or may jeopardize your long-term career goals.

Discuss these strategies with friends you trust. Evaluate them in light of your own personal situation before you decide which strategy(ies) to adopt. Only YOU can decide what's appropriate for you and your career future. Perhaps this list of strategies will stimulate your own creativity as you plan your future — inside or outside the Land of Penguins.

BLUE BIRD STRATEGY — Stay cheerful. Try to make the best of a difficult situation. You may be the kind of person who can put a positive spin on any situation. You are probably an optimist by nature, and you often see the good in other people, and you see the "silver lining in every cloud." This strategy can be quite effective, because you often get what you expect in terms of positive outcomes, and even when you don't, you know how to turn "lemons into lemonade"!

MOCKING BIRD STRATEGY — Mimic those around you. Work hard to be as much like them as you can so you'll fit in. People who adopt this strategy are good at assimilating into an organization — they are flexible and adaptable and can often fit in very well. This is a fine strategy and can lead to great career success. However, mocking birds need to be aware that the personal price they pay for adapting may be very high. Some people almost lead "double lives" — they act one way at work, and they can only relax and be themselves away from work. Think twice before you "sell your soul" to be successful.

SPARROW STRATEGY — Be neutral and try to blend into the background. Keep a low profile and nobody will notice you. This strategy can help you to survive for a long time and you may be happy flying through your career like this. You will probably survive many organizational dangers and threats. Since you don't stand out you probably will not be a target. But you may pay a price by never experiencing the exhilaration of contributing new ideas, taking risks, taking a stand on an important issue on which you have strong feelings, or gaining credibility and visibility for potential career advancement.

HUMMINGBIRD STRATEGY — Move fast; be efficient.
(It's hard to hit a moving target.) You can get a lot of mileage out of this strategy, and be quite successful in your organization and your career. You will probably be seen as a good worker who can be depended upon to produce quick results.

CANARY STRATEGY — Be colorful and charming; fit in by becoming the center of positive attention. Being charming and entertaining can take you a long way in life and in your work — especially in certain fields. This is a natural strategy for people in sales and marketing, public relations, and human resources, and it can be equally effective in many other fields as well. But be careful that you develop some "substance" to back up that "style." If you're "all fluff," people will figure that out sooner or later.

SWAN STRATEGY — Do your job and gain respect by being dignified. Some people command the respect of others by virtue of their impressive personal presence. They convey an image of natural poise and confidence. This often comes from a deep-seated sense of self-worth or demonstrated competence and skill. Swans can be very successful in their careers and in their lives.

VULTURE STRATEGY — Shrug off your differentness. Make yourself indispensable by doing the jobs nobody else wants to do. Every organization needs scavengers — people who will do the jobs that everyone else dislikes. You may take on the "mission impossible" projects that others are afraid to tackle; or you may willingly do the boring but important work that needs to get done. You can make yourself a key player in your organization by using this vulture strategy.

OWL STRATEGY — Become valuable and important by becoming an "expert" at something the organization needs. Every organization needs owls — technical specialists, subject matter experts, or simply thoughtful "old timers" who have a lot of organizational history and learning in their heads. You can make yourself an indispensable part of your group if you become an owl.

HAWK STRATEGY — Become valuable to the organization by being a skilled hunter — bringing in new business, new opportunities. Hawks are very valuable in any organization, and they are usually appreciated and treated very well, even if they are somewhat "different" from the mainstream. Your job security and your career success are a function of your ability to generate opportunities, new business, or growth in the organization. You'll do well.

DOVE STRATEGY — Become the peacemaker, the troubleshooter who solves problems. This is an important role, since all organizations experience conflicts or problems — in operations, in employee relations, in finance, in marketing, and in many other areas of work. If you are good at resolving conflicts, sorting out complex issues, and solving problems, you will be valued by your organization — by *any* organization!

EAGLE STRATEGY — Rise above the situation and play a leadership role in changing your organization for the better. It's not easy being an eagle. It often means ignoring your own feelings for the sake of a larger good, and making personal sacrifices that will benefit everyone in the long run. There is always a price for becoming a leader, but there are also great rewards. Do you want to be a leader in your organization? Can you make a contribution that will help make a better workplace with a strong future? If so, soar as fast and as high as your wings will carry you. The world needs more leaders!

PEACOCK STRATEGY — Dazzle others with your incredible talent and positive results. But be aware that others may be uncomfortable with your flash and dazzle, or they may be threatened by your success. Peacocks can be quite successful as superstars in any field, but it can sometimes backfire on them when other people are put off by their style. You may have to learn when to keep your feathers folded up modestly and when it's OK to flash them open for effect. Most people enjoy being around peacocks, but sometimes peacocks overdo a good thing (and it can turn into a bit of a problem). Some organizations (like penguin organizations) will not tolerate peacock behavior at all, so peacocks should be careful where they decide to work and how they may be required to change their behavior.

OSTRICH STRATEGY — Bury your head in the sand. Pretend nothing is wrong. This strategy may work for you for a while, but in the long run, it will probably not serve you well. Ignoring organizational realities can endanger your career potential and leave you open to getting blind-sided when you least expect it.

CHICKEN STRATEGY — Cower and complain about how awful things are, but don't venture forth to try to change things. You can see that there are problems in your organization — problems that have a negative impact on you. But you are too frightened or too insecure to take a risk to try to change things. This strategy may keep you "safe" but it will also add to your feelings of powerlessness and insignificance.

GOOSE STRATEGY — Cut your losses and fly south in search of a more hospitable environment. Sometimes what's important is to know when to cut your losses and move on. If there are "irreconcilable differences" between you and your organization (or you and your boss) and none of the other strategies seem workable to you, then leaving the organization might be your best option. This is a highly personal decision, and only you can decide if this is the right choice for you.

OTHER STRATEGIES — Be creative and write your own!

_____

_____

_____

_____

_____

_____

How You Can Tell if You Work in the Land of Penguins ...

1. Decision making emphasizes precedent, tradition, and control ("That's never been done before" or "That's against company policy") — *rather* than creativity, risk-taking, flexibility, and innovation ("Seems like a good idea — let's try it").

2. Excessive emphasis is placed on "chain of command" and "not rocking the boat." Loyalty to your boss (or other powerful people) is valued over loyalty to the organization or the customer.

3. Discussions are characterized by groupthink (little disagreement and debate), and by avoidance of confrontation or clash with tradition and the existing order.

4. It is extremely important to publicly adhere to the "company line" and be discrete in all conversations. You must be careful who you trust with your candid opinions, and *never* point out that "the Emperor has no clothes."

5. "Organizational constipation" makes *everything* move slowly. Very bureaucratic — several layers of approval required to launch new projects, resolve customer problems, purchase things, etc.

6. Subject to "analysis paralysis" — too many committees that study issues but have no authority to make decisions; low level of risk taking.

7. Organization has a tendency to *add* layers of management rather than eliminate them. Special jobs are created for the "fair-haired boys" (and girls) as grooming positions. Up and coming fast-trackers are simply younger versions of those already in power.

8. People refer to "the good ole boy system" as the way things get done and people get ahead. Promotions and plum assignments are based on who you know and being one of the "chosen ones" rather than on skill and ability.

9. Newcomers are encouraged to assimilate, conform, "fit in." Form is valued over content. Compatible style is often more important than results. Failure to fit in has dire consequences for one's career.

10. The top executives all look like they go to the same tailor and the same barber. Conservative bias in attire, thinking, and behavior.

11. Trappings of status and power are visible and prominent (i.e., executive dining rooms, executive cars, executive bathrooms, etc.). Excessive emphasis on rank and position within the organization.

12. Few women and ethnic minorities are in leadership positions. Those that *are* there are often the staunchest penguins of all, in order to prove their loyalty to the existing order.

Tips for Penguins Who Want to Change Themselves

1. Look at your own biases and attitudes — acknowledge them honestly to yourself and stay aware of them. Consciousness is the first step toward change.

2. Practice divergent thinking — there are many paths to success and many different ways to do things and accomplish results. Your way is only one way. Applaud creativity, innovation, and resourcefulness in others.

3. Try to separate style from substance. Don't get hung up on stylistic differences with others — keep your focus on substance, shared goals and objectives, and results.

4. Get out of your comfort zone. Go out of your way to spend time with people who are different from you. Invite an exotic bird to lunch, or other business/social events.

5. Be a visible role model to other penguins. People watch what you DO more than what you SAY. Incorporate exotic birds into your daily interactions and activities. Consider mentoring exotic birds, while allowing them to be themselves.

Tips for Penguins Who Want to Change Their Organizations

1. Recognize that the world is changing, and the future looks very different from the past. What worked in the past may now be obsolete. A new future requires new behaviors.

2. Create opportunities for exotic birds to contribute their talents and ideas — project teams, task forces, special projects.

3. Consider creating special advisory groups, advocacy groups, or support groups for people who consider themselves to be "different" in some fundamental way. Listen to them; engage in dialogue; involve them in finding ways to make the penguin culture more diversity-friendly.

4. Provide processes and resources to help people of ALL kinds deal with their feelings about the organization's culture — as it has been in the past, as it is today, and as it could be in the future. Make it safe to talk about fears and anxieties, hopes and aspirations.

5. Celebrate small successes — both individual and organizational. Change can be slow, bumpy, and uncomfortable. Reward the progress your organization makes. Keep up your commitment to change!

Additional Resources
for Peacocks *and* for Penguins

TRAINING MATERIALS & MERCHANDISE
available from:

XICOM
Woods Road
Tuxedo, New York 10987
800-759-4266 phone
914-351-4762 fax

"The Penguin Index: Assessing Management Practices and Diversity Acceptance in Your Organization"

Do you work in the Land of Penguins or the Land of Opportunity? This instrument is designed to assess your organization's culture and management practices. Simple (25 questions), easy to administer, works well in training seminars or as an employee survey. Includes strategies for management and strategies for employees.

"The Peacock Profile: Assessing Individual Uniqueness and Organizational 'Fit'"

How well do you "fit" in your organization? This simple, clear, 25-question instrument assesses the fit between individuals and their jobs and organizations. Includes discussion questions, various strategies, and action planning for individuals.

"Peacocks and Penguins: Facilitator's Guide for Your Journey to the Land of Opportunity"

A comprehensive manual, including how to use the instruments in training seminars, employee surveys, and career coaching. Complete with several training designs, handouts, classroom exercises, overhead transparency masters, and a thorough bibliography of books, videos, audiotapes, journal articles, and additional resources.

"Birds of a Feather" Game

This delightful game is both instructional and entertaining. Designed for use with groups of all sizes, the game incorporates the principles of openness, tolerance, flexibility, and willingness to learn from others who are different. Questions test participants' responses to various situations, and colorful "feathers" are awarded for creative answers that value the creativity of diversity. Comes complete with game book, game materials for players, and a one-hour audiotape of valuable content materials for use by the game facilitator.

"Celebrate Diversity!" T-shirts

Colorful T-shirts silk screened with one of the most popular images from the book, a gathering of many different birds under the banner of "E Pluribus Maximus" (Greatness from Many). T-shirts are white, with six-color silk screen design. Available on an individual basis, or volume purchase for diversity training programs.

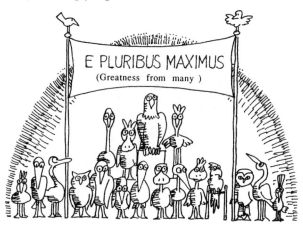

"Magic" Penguin and Peacock Coffee Mugs

These unusual coffee mugs show a row of penguins against a dark blue background. When you pour in hot liquid, the blue background magically turns transparent, revealing a glorious Perry the Peacock with the words "Show Your True Colors" among his tail feathers. A practical, every-day reminder of the message of being valued for who you really are.

ANIMATED TRAINING VIDEO available from:

CRM Films
2215 Faraday Avenue
Carlsbad, California 92008
800-421-0833 phone
619-931-5792 fax

"A Peacock in the Land of Penguins" (11 minutes)

Video comes with a Leader's Guide, which includes background on diversity and empowerment, training designs, exercises, and a bibliography.

For **seminars, keynote speeches, workshops, and consulting services** by
"BJ" Hateley and **Warren H. Schmidt,** please contact:

PEACOCK PRODUCTIONS
701 Danforth Drive
Los Angeles, California 90065

213-227-6205 phone
213-227-0705 fax
peacockHQ@aol.com

— BJ Hateley —

BJ Hateley is in many ways like the lead character in this fable — colorful and extravagant, noisy and messy — a bird who is difficult to ignore. She is a free spirit who loves her work — a child of the 60's, who sees her mission in life as "comforting the afflicted, and afflicting the comfortable" (a line she once heard in a good sermon). She does both of them very well — especially the latter. She is a human potential missionary who hangs out in corporations and other organizations, showing people how they can do well by doing good.

Her USC doctoral studies in Social Ethics equipped her to be a professional do-gooder, while her years in the business world taught her to speak the language of the bottom line. She considers herself to be a pragmatic idealist. Her undergraduate training in the social sciences taught her to observe, listen, ask good questions, and analyze human behavior in all its complexity and paradoxes — great preparation for a life in business!

BJ was reluctant to leave the academic nest (she wanted to be a professor when she grew up), and spent seven years on the staff at USC — her last position there was Director of Staff Training and Professional Development. While she was supposed to be writing her dissertation she published a pop psychology/pop religion book called *Telling Your Story, Exploring Your Faith* (it paid better and was more fun).

She finally decided to try her wings in the "real world" of business, and landed at *The Los Angeles Times,* where she spent almost five years as the Manager of Training and Development. It was at the newspaper that she developed a keen interest in studying other types of "birds," and she learned a lot while directing training programs and consulting projects for the company. She left *The Times* in 1991 to form her own consulting and training company, Steps to Success.

Like any good peacock, BJ loves an audience, and is a popular workshop leader and public speaker. She really shows her true colors when she's talking about some of her favorite subjects: workforce diversity, leadership skills and success strategies for women, motivation, communication, sexual harassment, management development, and her all-time favorite — how to manage your boss! She also consults with organizations on other human resource issues — teambuilding, employee surveys, strategic planning, etc. She has managed to put on her penguin suit often enough to work with many respectable corporate and nonprofit clients, ranging from the Chrysler Corporation and Southern California Edison to the American Press Institute, Planned Parenthood, and the American Lung Association.

This irridescent and irrepressible bird is a Southern California native, and is one of the rare people who really loves L.A. She is the proud mom to Michael, a soon-to-be-famous young rock star (what else would you expect in L.A.?) Her favorite song is "I Gotta Be Me."

BJ Hateley can be contacted at:

Peacock Productions
701 Danforth Drive
Los Angeles, California 90065
Phone: (213) 227-6205
Email: BJHpeacock@aol.com

— Warren H. Schmidt —

Warren Schmidt looks like a penguin and likes to think of himself as a peacock. He's really quite advanced in years ("chronologically gifted" he calls it) but has six grandchildren who force him to keep playing basketball, baseball, and tennis as if he were only middle-aged.

In his long career Warren has played many roles — from minister to psychologist, from professor to city commissioner, from researcher to screen writer. He has taught others how to do Life Planning, but his own career has been shaped by a lot of unexpected opportunities — leading him from Detroit, Michigan (where he was born), to Missouri, to New York, to Massachusetts, to Ohio, to Washington, D.C. — and finally to settle down in the San Fernando Valley in California with his family of one wife (Reggie) and four kids (now increased to a clan of sixteen). While in California he has taught at two of that state's great educational institutions, UCLA and USC. Even when he "settled down" at UCLA, however, he didn't stay with a single role, moving from the psychology department to the Graduate School of Management, where he ended up as dean of executive education. After twenty-two years, however, Warren finally became a mature, dependable professor of public administration at the University of Southern California (but not quite a penguin, he insists!)

Warren likes to write — particularly with someone else. He first tasted the fun of collaboration when he and Bob Tannenbaum wrote an article on "How to Choose a Leadership Pattern" for the *Harvard Business Review* — a management classic that has sold more than one million reprints. He has written books on teamwork with Gordon Lippitt and Paul Buchanan, monographs on managerial values with Barry Posner, and most recently, two books on Total Quality Management with Jerry Finnigan of the Xerox Corporation: *The Race Without a Finish Line* and *TQManager*. When BJ Hateley and Warren teamed up to write this Peacock tale, it began another delightful creative partnership that became even more interesting when Sam Weiss got into the act!

A major dimension was added to Warren's life in 1969 when he wrote a parable about divisiveness in America titled "Is It Always Right to Be Right?" Its appearance in *The Los Angeles Times* attracted the attention of four film producers (as well as Ted Kennedy and Spiro Agnew). Steven Bosustow (of Mr. Magoo fame) made an animated film of the parable; Orson Welles narrated it — and it won an Academy Award in 1971. As an "instant expert" on films, Warren was invited to become an advisor for CRM Films — and has never stopped writing and advising. CRM Films produced an animated video of Warren and BJ's *A Peacock in the Land of Penguins* in 1995, and they are currently at work on a sequel, tentatively titled *Pigeon Holed in the Land of Penguins*.

Warren teaches an occasional course at USC and continues to speak, consult, and conduct seminars through his little company, Chrysalis, Inc.

Chrysalis, Inc.
9238 Petit Avenue
Northridge, California 91343
Phone: (818) 892-3092
Email: wschmidt@UCLA.edu

— Sam Weiss —

Sam is a distinguished dropout of both the Rhode Island School of Design and the Art Center College of Design. Their deans tried to convince him to stay and finish school, but his calling was elsewhere — he had pictures to draw and films to make.

He brings a unique artistic style to the illustration of books and other print materials, adding a charm all his own. With the touch of a pen, characters come to life — with the stroke of a paintbrush, whole worlds begin to unfold. In addition to being a versatile artist, he is also a musician, film director, script writer, and all-round creative spirit.

Sam is probably best known as one of the preeminent directors in the animation industry. He has written and/or directed numerous business-oriented training videos, including *The Winds of Change, To Try Again and Succeed, That's Not My Problem, I Told Them Exactly How To Do It,* and *The Race Without a Finish Line.* His most recent production is *A Peacock in the Land of Penguins* for CRM Films. He is currently directing the film adaptation of *A Complaint is a Gift* for ETC.

The films he has directed have been honored all over the world, including an Academy Award nomination for *The Legend of John Henry,* sung by Roberta Flack with music by Herbie Hancock, and a Television Academy Emmy for *The Wrong Way Kid* (which included four adapted children's books). He has won the Gold Award of the Art Directors Club of New York, Outstanding Film of the Year at the London Film Festival, First Prize at Zagreb International Film Festival, the Jack London Award, and numerous other awards and honors.

Sam Weiss began his career as Art Director and Designer on the Mr. Magoo and Bullwinkle shows, and within a few years was directing one of the hottest animated series of the late '60s, *Hot Wheels.* He moved on to Bosustow Entertainment, where he directed more than fifty films, including four CBS one-hour specials, which required adapting thirty children's books to animation. He also produced and directed thirty-five G.I. Joe's for Marvel and was a Seqence Director on the critically acclaimed Little Nemo animated feature.

During his career he has directed the voice talents of Carol Burnett, Alan Arkin, James Earl Jones, Milton Berle, Rob Reiner, Mickey Rooney, Stan Freberg, Patrick Stewart, and other notable actors and singers.

Sam and his wonderful wife Marjorie make their home in Santa Monica, California.

Requests for his autograph can be directed to:

Sam Weiss Productions
401 Sycamore Road
Santa Monica, California 90402
Phone: (310) 459-8838